George Washington Carver

The Peanut Scientist

Patricia and Fredrick McKissack

Illustrated by Ned O.

❖ *Great African Americans Series* ❖

Enslow Publishers, Inc.

44 Fadem Road	PO Box 38
Box 699	Aldershot
Springfield, NJ 07081	Hants GU12 6BP
USA	UK

To Margaret Emily Haskins

Library of Congress Cataloging-in-Publication Data

McKissack, Pat 1944-
　　George Washington Carver: the peanut scientist / Patricia and
Fredrick McKissack : illustrated by Ned O.
　　　　p. cm. — (Great African Americans series)
　　Summary: Simple text and illustrations describe the life and
accomplishments of the scientist who promoted the idea of crop
rotation and found many uses for peanuts.
　　ISBN 0-89490-308-X
　　1. Carver, George Washington, 1864?–1943—Juvenile literature.
2. Afro-American agriculturists—Biography—Juvenile literature.
3. Agriculturists—United States—Biography—Juvenile literature.
4. Peanuts—Juvenile literature. [1. Carver, George Washington,
1864?–1943. 2. Agriculturists. 3. Afro-Americans—Biography.]
I. McKissack, Fredrick. II. Ostendorf, Edward, ill. III. Title.
IV. Series: McKissack, Pat, 1944–　Great African American series.
S417.C3M298　1991
630'.92—dc20
[B]　　　　　　　　　　　　　　　　　　91-8814
　　　　　　　　　　　　　　　　　　　　CIP
　　　　　　　　　　　　　　　　　　　　AC

Printed in the United States of America

10 9 8 7 6 5

Photo credits: Library of Congress, pp. 4, 10, 12, 14; Patricia McKissack, p. 27;
Moorland-Spingarn Research Center, Howard University, p. 24; George Washington
Carver National Monument, p. 20.

Illustration credits: Ned O., pp. 6, 7, 8, 15, 16, 17, 18, 19, 22, 26, 28.
Cover Illustration: Ned O.

Contents

George Washington Carver
Born: Between 1860 and 1864, Diamond Grove, Missouri.
Died: January 5, 1943, Tuskegee, Alabama.

1

Stolen in the Night

Moses and Susan Carver owned a small farm in Diamond Grove, Missouri. They owned one **slave**,* Mary. She had two small children, James and George.

One day a neighbor came to warn the Carvers. Slave **raiders** were in the area. Slave raiders stole slaves and sold them again.

The raiders came late that night. They

---

* Words in **bold type** are explained in *Words to Know* on page 30.

stole Mary and baby George, and rode away. Moses Carver went after them. They found baby George by the side of the road. They never found Mary.

The Carvers had no children. So they raised James and George as their own. The boys called the Carvers Aunt Susan and Uncle Moses.

George was a sickly boy. His voice was thin and weak. He **stuttered** sometimes

when he spoke in a hurry. But he was a happy child who loved plants and animals.

Aunt Susan taught him to read and write. She gave him a Bible. He loved his Bible very much.

The boy was always full of questions. He wanted to learn about everything. But the only school for black children was miles away. It was too far for a little boy to walk each day. George had to wait.

2

Why? and How?

When George was about twelve years old, he left the Carvers. He wanted to go to school. He walked to Neosho, Missouri. A family found George sleeping in their barn. They let the boy live with them. George worked and went to Lincoln School.

A few years passed. George learned all he could at Lincoln. He heard about a school in Fort Scott, Kansas. So he moved there. Another family let George live with them. Soon, young Carver was old enough to live on his own. For a while he moved from place to place.

Then he came to a small Kansas town. Another George Carver lived there too. So George added a "W" to his name. "It is for Washington," he told his friends. *George*

George Carver (bottom right) wanted to be an artist. He studied art for a while. Some of his paintings hang in the Carver Museum in Tuskegee, Alabama.

Washington Carver—he liked the sound of his new name.

George wanted to go to **college**. Not many black men went to college in the 1890s. But George Carver was sure that he would go. He worked hard and saved his money.

At last Carver went to college in Iowa. There he studied what he liked best— plants and farming. Then he went to **Iowa State College** in Ames to study. He **graduated** in 1896. Still, there was much more he wanted to learn.

George Washington Carver would spend the rest of his life asking questions and looking for the answers. He was a **scientist**. And scientists are always asking: Why? and How?

Carver was asked to be in charge of the greenhouses at Iowa State College. It was a very good job offer. But another offer came from Tuskegee, Alabama. It was hard to choose.

3

Tuskegee Farm

George Carver was asked to stay at Iowa State and teach. But Booker T. Washington asked **Professor** Carver to come teach at **Tuskegee College** in Alabama.

The all-black school was started by Mr. Washington in 1881. In 1896, Mr. Washington wrote Professor Carver: "Will you come to Tuskegee to teach?" Carver thought about it. Then he answered: "I am coming."

It was fall 1896 when Professor Carver went to Tuskegee. He had 13 students. His job was to teach science. But he had no **lab**. This didn't stop him. The class made a lab from things they found.

The school also had a farm. The soil was poor. The cotton plants were small and

The students at Tuskegee helped to build their lab.

weak. Farmers in the South had been growing cotton on the land for many years. Professor Carver said, "The soil needs a rest." He and the class did a project. "We will not plant cotton," he said. "We will plant sweet potatoes. And they did.

The next year they grew **cowpeas**. "The land has to rest," he said. So the third year they grew cotton again. That cotton **crop** grew bigger and stronger than before. Carver was one of the first scientists to teach **crop rotation**.

The **boll weevil** is a bug that eats cotton plants. In the early 1900s boll weevils came into the United States from Mexico. Farmers were worried. What could they do? Carver told them to plant **goobers**! Boll weevils don't like goobers.

BULLETIN NO. 31   JUNE 1925

How to Grow the Peanut and 105 Ways of Preparing it for Human Consumption

Seventh Edition
January 1940

By
GEORGE W. CARVER, M. S. in AGR.
Director

EXPERIMENTAL STATION
TUSKEGEE INSTITUTE
Tuskegee Institute, Alabama

Professor Carver wrote books showing the many ways people could use the peanut, the sweet potato, and other plants.

4

Plant Goobers!

Goobers!

Goober is an old African name for peanut. Slaves brought goobers from Africa. They grew them in small gardens. Goobers were mostly used to feed animals.

Farmers came to Tuskegee from all over the South. Professor Carver told them about his work. What can be done with peanuts? They are only good for hogs.

Carver found many ways to use peanuts. His students liked peanut butter best.

Who will buy the peanuts? Professor Carver didn't know. But, like always, he kept looking for answers.

Then an idea came. The quiet professor asked a group of important **businessmen** to have dinner with him. He served them bread, soup, meat, cookies, and ice cream.

They all agreed that the food was good—very good. Then Professor Carver told them: Everything they had eaten had been made with peanuts! What a surprise!

Professor Carver was full of more surprises. He showed the businessmen what they could make from the peanuts. He showed them why they should buy the farmers' peanut crops. What he said made sense. Now the farmers could sell their crops.

It is no surprise that George Washington Carver was called the farmer's best friend.

Dr. Carver enjoyed his work so much. Sometimes he forgot to cash
his paychecks. He didn't own a suit. His friends bought him one.
They wanted him to look nice when he received a special award.

5

The Wizard of Tuskegee

George Washington Carver won many **awards**. Henry Ford, who made cars, gave him money to build a new lab. Every day scientists from many countries came to see "the **Wizard** of Tuskegee." Most of the time they found the small, quiet man working.

Professor Carver could have made lots of money. But owning things wasn't important to the great scientist. He owned one suit. And he walked to his lab every day.

Although he had no wife or children, he was never alone. Tuskegee was home. His students were family. When Professor Carver wasn't working, he enjoyed

reading the Bible Susan Carver had given him long ago.

The kind scientist everybody called "Prof" died on January 5, 1943. In 1946 the United States **Congress** named January 5th "George Washington Carver Day." He had given the world 300 ways to

Today people can visit the George Washington Carver museum at Tuskegee University in Alabama.

use the peanut and 118 ways to usc the sweet potato.

President Jimmy Carter, who was a peanut farmer from Georgia, said, "George Washington Carver was a great friend of the American farmer. He was a true genius."

Words to Know

award—An honor given to a person for doing something special.

boll weevil—A small bug that kills cotton plants.

businessmen—Those who own a company, factory or store.

college—A school beyond high school.

Congress—Government representatives and senators from each state who form a law-making body.

cowpeas—A vegetable that is related to the black-eyed pea.

crop—The plants a farmer grows during one season.

crop rotation—Ways to rest the soil by not planting a crop on it for several years or by growing different crops.

goobers—An old African name for peanuts.

graduate (GRAJ-uh-wait)—To finish all the studies at a school.

Iowa State College—A college founded in 1858, now called Iowa State University of Science and Technology.

lab—A short name for laboratory. A laboratory is a place where scientists work and study.

president (PREZ-i-dent)—The leader of a country or group.

professor—A name for a teacher who works at a college.

raiders—Another word for robbers.

scientist (SY-en-tist)—A person who studies about a subject by asking questions and then trying to find answers.

slave—A person who is owned by another. That person can be bought or sold.

stutter—To stumble over words.

Tuskegee College—A college founded in 1881 to teach African-American students. It is now called Tuskegee University.

wizard—A person who has super powers of knowledge.

Index